MY BOOK OF Spelling

GREG BLACKMAN
Dip. Teach., BEd., M.A. (Ed.), MACE.

**SELECT
EDITIONS**

OTHER TITLES IN THIS SERIES:

My Book of Interesting Facts

My Book of Tables

My Book of Grammar

My Book of Simple Maths

SELECT EDITIONS

This edition distributed by Selectabook Ltd
Folly Road, Roundway, Devizes
Wiltshire, England, SN 10 2HR

© The Book Company International, Australia 1996

First printed in 1996
Reprinted in 1997, 1998

ISBN 1863093028

Designed by Robyn Latimer
Printed in Hong Kong

Contents

Introduction

Spelling can be a difficult subject for a great many children. However, it is a very important, if not critical, part of writing. The best way to learn how to spell is to be given a good background in the English language and its spelling rules.

This book gives a basic introduction to how words are formed and the most frequently used spelling rules, with activities to complete for practice.

At the back of the book is a space to create a personal dictionary. This will become a very important resource.

Answers are also provided at the back of the book.

How To Use a Dictionary

Dictionaries are one of the most important resources for spelling. A good dictionary will give you the correct spelling of the base word and common suffixes. It will give the various meanings and show how to pronounce the word.

All children should be encouraged to use a dictionary whenever they are writing.

The Best Way to Learn

It has been proven that the

Look - Say - Cover - Write - Check

method is one of the best ways to learn how to spell a word. Each word is learnt individually by doing the following:

Look - Look at the word. Try to remember what the word looks like.

Say - Say the word out loud.

Cover - Cover up the word and try to picture it in your mind.

Write - Write the word.

Check - Check your spelling against the correct spelling. If the word is not right start again.

Other things you can do include:
• Think about the meaning of the word.
• Think about the sounds of the word.
• Try to write clearly.
• Don't be afraid to misspell words. Have a go!
• Practice proofreading.
• Look at the patterns of the letters within the words.
• Get help from other sources like dictionaries, thesauruses, personal lists, and other people who are good spellers. Dictionaries are the best resource.

Vowels and Consonants

Our language is based on twenty-six letters which are split into two groups, vowels and consonants. The vowels are: **a, e, i, o, u.** The consonants are all other letters.

All words must contain a vowel. The letter **y** is sometimes counted as a vowel because it can make the **i** vowel sound. Most of these words are short words and don't contain any other vowels. For example: try, cry.

Activity
Above each letter write a **v** for a vowel or a **c** for a consonant above each letter of the following words:

v c c v c v c c
activity

hockey

boy

aunt

face

kind

straight

baby

girl

great

magic

glass

football

school

father

together

various

unhappy

6

Silent Letters

Many words have silent letters. This means the sound of these letters are not pronounced. Some silent letters can affect the sounds of other letters. An **e** at the end of a word changes a previous short vowel to a long vowel.

Example

cat   **a** sound is short.

cāke   **a** sound is long.

Silent letters can appear anywhere in a word. Other silent letters include:

k	knock
b	lamb
h	ghost
p	psalm
n	hymn
t	listen
c	scissors
g	gnome
w	wrist

Activity

Underline the silent letter in these words.

knight   thumb   comb   column

Morphographs

All words are made up of morphographs.
A morphograph is a part of a word that has meaning.
Some words have only one morphograph while
others have more than one.

All morphographs have meaning. Under-standing
morphographs makes our spelling rules easier to
understand.

The following words have only one morphograph:

doubt	real	mother
create	image	athlete.

These words have more than one morphograph.

unkind = un + kind   quickly = quick + ly
misspell = mis + spell   childish = child + ish
forever = for + ever   surround= sur + round
foolishly = fool + ish + ly

Activity
Decide if these words have one, or more than one
morphograph.

builder	view	powerful
cure	moveable	beauty

Prefixes

A prefix is a morphograph added to the beginning of a word. As all morphographs have meaning, the new word must have a different meaning. Below is some prefixes with their meanings.

Position

fore - before or in front
inter - between
mid - middle
out - beyond
pre - before
re - back, again
under - beneath
up - upwards

not

dis - not
im - not
in - not
un - not

Others

en - to make
un - opposite of
mono - one, single, alone

Activity

a) Complete these words by adding a prefix.

. . happy   . . complete   . . . night

b) Underline the prefix in these words.

invisible   outlaw   unable   underfed   redo

Suffixes

A suffix is a morphograph added to the end of a word. As all morphographs have meaning, the new word must have a different meaning. Below is some suffixes with their meanings .

can do, able
-able - can do, able
-ible - can do, able

one who
-er (to a verb) - one who
-ist - one who
-or (to a verb) - one who

Others
-al - belonging to
-en - make
-er - from ish - comparison
-less - without
-less - lack of, alone
-ness - state of being
-ward - direction
-y - like

full of
-ful - full of
-ous - full of

Activity
a) Complete these words by adding a suffix.

care _ _ _ _   football _ _   chill _   tough _ _

b) Underline the suffix in these words.

acceptable   cyclist   governor   dangerous

Drop the 'e' Rule

When a word ends in a silent **e,** drop the **e** when adding a suffix that begins with a vowel.

Example

  race + ing = racing

Activity

1. Underline each of the words in column A that ends in a silent **e.**
2. Write a small **c** or **v** above the first letter in column B depending if it is a consonant or a vowel.
3. Now join the base word and the suffix, making sure you use the rule.

Column A		Column B		Final Word
		v		
<u>dance</u>	+	ing	=	dancing
fashion	+	able	=	
make	+	ing	=	
pure	+	est	=	
power	+	ful	=	
race	+	ed	=	

Be careful there are exceptions to this rule.
eg. courageous

Doubling Rule

When adding a suffix beginning with a vowel to the end of a short word that ends in a consonant, vowel, consonant, double the last consonant.

Example

  step + ing = stepping
  shop + er = shopper

Activity

1. Write a small **c** or **v** above the last three letters in column A. Underline each of the words that are short words (4 letters or less) and end in consonant, vowel, consonant.
2. Write a small **c** or **v** above the first letter in column B depending if it is a consonant or vowel.
3. Now join the morphographs in Column A and B making sure you use the rule.

Column A		Column B		Final Word
c v c		v		
swim	+	ing	=	swimming
mad	+	ly	=	
join	+	ing	=	
stop	+	ed	=	
mud	+	y	=	
pain	+	ful	=	

12

Changing the 'y' to 'i' Rule

When a word ends in a consonant and a **y** and you are adding a suffix that begins with anything except an **i** you must change the **y** to an **i**.

Example

study + ed = studied	funny + er = funnier
carry + ing = carrying	marry + age = marriage

Activity

1. Write a small **c** or **v** above the last two letters in column A. Underline each of the words that end in consonant and a **y**.
2. Decide if the first letter in column B is an **i**.
3. Now join the morphographs in Column A and B making sure you use the rule.

Column A		Column B		Final Word
cc				
<u>happy</u>	+	er	=	happier
merry	+	est	=	
pity	+	ful	=	
play	+	ful	=	

Rule for Making Plurals

Plural means more than one. We use plurals when we want to talk about more than one object.

Example

  cat - cats   race - races   bush - bushes

There are a number of rules that help you spell the plurals of words.

Rule One

Most plurals are made by adding a **s** to singular nouns.

Example

  dog - dogs   road - roads   board - boards

Activity

Make the following words plural by adding **s** to the end of the word.

dance -   desk -   book -

mask -   football -   pen -

key -   chair -   stick -

Rule Two

Words ending in **s, x, z, ch, sh,** consonant and **o,** are made plural by adding **es** after the word.

Example

pass - passes   box - boxes

buzz - buzzes   mosquito -mosquitoes

church - churches   rich - riches

Activity

a) Make the following words plural by adding **es** to the end of the word.

brush -	peach -	dish -
pass -	echo -	match -
guess -	fox -	business -
tomato -	suffix -	

b) However, there are exceptions to this rule. For example, piano - pianos. Can you find three others.

1. _____ 2. _____ 3. _____

Rule Three

Words ending in **f** or **fe** are made plural by changing the **f** or **fe** to a **v** and adding **es.**

Example

   calf - calves   knife - knives

However, there are exceptions to this rule. For example, belief - beliefs. Can you find three others.

a) 1._____ 2. _____ 3. _____

Activity

b) Make the following words plural by using the rule.

wolf -	calf -	loaf-
life -	wife -	shelf -
scarf -	relief -	thief -
loaf -	self -	leaf -

Rule Four

This rule relates back to the **v** to **i** rule. When a word ends in a consonant and a **y**, we change the **y** to an **i** and add **es** to the word to make it plural.

Example

  baby - babies   fly - flies   lady- ladies

Activity

a) Make the following words plural by changing the **y** to **i** and adding **es** to the end of the word.

fairy -   spy -   carry -

try -   marry -   rally -

When a word ends in a vowel and a **y**, add **s** to the word to make it plural.

Example

  toy - toys   donkey - donkeys

b) Make the following words plural by adding **s** to the end of the word.

play-   valley -   stay-

joy -   display -   way -

Rule Five

Some words in our language change completely when the plural is made.

Example

mouse - mice   tooth - teeth

I - we   she - they

Activity

a) What is the plural of these words.

man   _____

goose   _____

myself   _____

Other words do not change at all for the plural.

Example

fish   sheep

Activity

b) Can you find three others.

1._____ 2._____ 3._____

Adding 'full' to a Word Rule

When the suffix **full** is added to a word you drop one **l**.
Example
waste + ful = wasteful   truth + ful =truthful

Activity
Add **full** to the following words.

thought -   peace -   use -
delight -   rest -   wonder -

'i' Before 'e' except After 'c' Rule

When the sound is **eeee** you write **ie** except after **c**.
Example
niece   believe   chief   fierce

Activity
a) Complete these words.

br . . f   f . . ld   rec . . pt   p . . ce

Be careful as there are exceptions to the rule.
Example
seize

Adding 'y' to Words Ending in 'l'

Double the **l** when adding **y** to a word ending in **l**.

Example

usual - usually   peaceful - peacefully

Activity

Add **y** to these words.

natural -   normal -

beautiful -   special -

truthful -   playful -

Antonyms

Words that are opposite in meaning are called antonyms.

short - long   dirty - clean   rich - poor

Activity
a) Write an antonym for each of the following words:

black -   ugly -   small -

Sometimes antonyms are formed by using a prefix.

Activity
b) By using a prefix, write the opposite of these words.

possible

honest

happy

roll

stable

stick

Synonyms

Words that are similar in meaning are called synonyms.

neat - tidy   middle - centre   house - home

Activity
a) Write a synonym for each of the following words:
level -   short -   gift -

b) Using the sentence below, write five synonyms for **said.**

"Here I am," said the girl.

1. _____

2. _____

3. _____

4. _____

5. _____

Thesauruses are a great resource for finding synonyms.

Homonyms

Words that sound the same but have different meanings and sometimes spelling. This is a list of the most common.

to - two - too

here - hear

buy - by

peace - piece

way - weigh

our - hour

right - write

pray - prey

days - daze

straight - strait

plain - plane

lone - loan

birth - berth

bored - board

hole - whole

quay - key

main - mane

their - there - they're

wear - where - we're

pair - pear

ate - eight

its - it's

scent - sent - cent

thrown - throne

vain - vein

allowed - aloud

past - passed

wine- whine

cereal - serial

alter - altar

minor - miner

rows - rose

seen - scene

pain - pane

Activity

a) Write a homonym for the following words and the meanings of each word:

meet -

maid -

Contractions

A contraction is a word that is shortened by leaving letters out, replacing them with an apostrophe.
This is a list of the most common contractions. The apostrophe indicates where the letters have been left out.

can't - can not   couldn't - could not
didn't - did not   doesn't - does not
he'd - he had   he'll - he will
he's - he is   how's - how is
I'd - I had   I'll - I will
isn't - is not   shan't - shall not
she'd - she had   they're - they are
we'd - we had   we've - we have
what's - what is   who's - who is
who've - who have   won't - will not
you'll - you will   you're - you are

Activity

a) Place the apostrophe in the correct place for these contractions and write the letter/s left out.

wasnt -   theres -   theyve -

b) Write the contraction for the following.

can not -   will not -   it is -

24

Anagrams

When a new word is made by changing the letters in another word it is called an anagram.

palm - lamp   lain - nail   fibre - brief

Activity
a) Underline the words that are anagrams of the first word.

palms   lamps, plums, psalm

paces   cares, capes, space

races   scare, cases, cares

b) Make anagrams from these words.

range - (mad) _ _ _ _ _

lump - (fruit) _ _ _ _

sauce - (reason) _ _ _ _ _

salt - (position) _ _ _ _

inch - (part of the face) _ _ _ _

Commonly Misspelt Words

These words are commonly misspelt by primary aged children. By the time they leave primary school they should be able to spell the following words.

accident	everything	new	tonight
answers	February	nineteen	too
any	foreign	none	tough
beautiful	forty	often	trouble
been	friend	once	truly
beginning	government	our	Tuesday
believe	half	pieces	two
built	hoping	photograph	used
business	horse	physical	very
busy	hour	raise	wear
buy	how	ready	weather
can't	instead	said	Wednesday
choose	island	says	were
clothes	its	scientist	when
colour	it's	seems	where
competition	just	separate	whether
cough	knew	shoes	which
could	knowledge	since	who
country	laid	some	whole
dying	lose	straight	whose
disappear	loose	sure	women
disappoint	magic	tear	won't
does	making	there	would
done	many	their	write
don't	meant	they	writing
early	minute	though	wrote
environment	much	through	
every	necessary	tired	

My Dictionary

Use this space to create your own dictionary. Put in words that you have misspelt or had to check in a dictionary and are likely to use again. You can also include interesting words, words that trick you and unusual words from other subjects that you will have to use. The more words you add to this dictionary the more helpful it will be.

A a

accident
answers
any

B b

beautiful
been
beginning
believe
built
business
busy
buy

C c

can't
choose
clothes
colour
competition
cough
could
country

D d

dying
disappear
disappoint
does
done
don't

E e

early
environment
every
everything

F f

February
foreign
forty
friend

G g

government

H h

half
hoping
horse
hour
how

I i

instead
island
its
it's

J j

just

K k

knew
knowledge

L l

laid
lose
loose

M m

magic
making
many
meant
minute
much

N n

necessary
new
nineteen

O o

often

once

our

P p

pieces
photograph
physical

Q q

queen

R r

raise
ready

S s

said
says
scientist
seems
separate
shoes
since
some
straight
sure

T t

tear
there
their
they
though
through
tired
tonight
too
tough
trouble
truly
Tuesday
two

U u

used

V v

very

W w

wear
weather
Wednesday
were
when
where
whether
which
who
whole
whose
women

won't
would
write
writing
wrote

X x

xerox

Y y

yacht

Z z

zebra

Answers

Answers not found in this section should not necessarily be discounted as not every possibility has been included in this section because of limited space.

Vowels and Consonants

c c c v v c c c	c v v c c v c c	c v c c v c	c v c c	c c c v v c
s t r a i g h t	f o o t b a l l	h o c k e y	b a b y	s c h o o l

c v c	c v c c	c v c c v c	v v c c	c c v v c
b o y	g i r l	f a t h e r	a u n t	g r e a t

c v c v c c v c	c v c v	c v c v c	c v c v v v c	c v c c
t o g e t h e r	f a c e	m a g i c	v a r i o u s	k i n d

c c v c c	v c c v c c c
g l a s s	u n h a p p y

Silent Letters

<u>k</u>night   thum<u>b</u>   com<u>b</u>   colum<u>n</u>

Morphographs

builder - build + er (2), view - view (1) , powerful - power + ful (2) , cure - cure (1), moveable - move + able (2), use - use (1)

Prefixes

a) unhappy, incomplete, midnight.
b) <u>in</u>visible   <u>out</u>law   <u>un</u>able   <u>un</u>derfed   <u>re</u>do

Suffixes

a) careless, footballer, chilly, toughen.
b) accept<u>able</u>, cycl<u>ist</u>, govern<u>or</u>, danger<u>ous</u>

Drop the 'e' Rule

        v   v

fashion + able = fashionable   <u>make</u> + ing = making

      v   c   v

<u>pure</u> + est = purest   power + ful = powerful   <u>race</u> + ed = raced

Doubling Rule

c v c cc   vvc v   cvc   v

<u>mad</u> + ly = madly   join + ing = joining   <u>stop</u> + ed = stopped

c vc   c (vowel sound) vvc c

<u>mud</u> + y = muddy   pain + ful = painful

Changing the 'y' to 'i' Rule

  cc   cc   vc

<u>merry</u> + est = merriest   <u>pity</u> + ful = pitiful   play + ful = playful

Rule for Making Plurals

Rule One   dance - dances; desk - desks; book - books; mask - masks; football - footballs; pen - pens; key - keys; chair - chairs; stick - sticks

Rule Two   a) brush - bushes; peach - peaches; dish - dishes; pass - passes; echo - echoes; match - matches; guess - guesses; fox - foxes; business - businesses; tomato - tomatoes; suffix - suffixes

b) banjos, silos, solos, duos, merinos, altos, radios, studios, rodeos, folios, kangaroos, photos

Rule Three   a) proof, dwarf, roof, bluff, gulf, handkerchief, strife, cliff, staff, reef

b) wolf - wolves; calf - calves; loaf- loaves; life - lives; wife - wives; shelf - shelves; scarf - scarves; relief - relieves; thief - thieves; loaf - loaves; self - selves; leaf - leaves

Rule Four   a) fairy - fairies; spy - spies; carry - carries; try - tries; marry - marries; rally - rallies

b) play - plays; valley - valleys; stay - stays; joy - joys; display - displays; way - ways

Rule Five   a) man - men, goose - geese, myself - ourselves

b) deer, cod, trout, salmon, reindeer, cannon, innings

Adding 'full' to a Word Rule

thought - thoughtful, peace - peaceful, use - useful,
delight - delightful, rest - restful, wonder - wonderful

'i' Before 'e' except After 'c' Rule

a) brief, field, receipt, piece

Adding 'y' to Words Ending in 'l'

natural - naturally, normal - normally, beautiful - beautifully,
special - specially, truthful - truthfully, playful - playfully

Antonyms

a) black - white; ugly - beautiful; small - large.
b) possible - impossible, honest - dishonest, happy - unhappy, roll -
   unroll, stable - unstable, stick - unstick

Synonyms

a)level - flat, plane; short - little, brief; gift - present,donation, grant
b) cried, yelled, shouted, moaned, sighed, whispered

Homonyms

a) meet - meat, maid - made

Contractions

a) wasnt - wasn't (o), theres - there's (i), theyve - they've (ha).
b) can not - can't, will not - won't, it is - it's

Anagrams

a) palms   lamps, plums, psalm
    paces   cares, capes, space
    races   scare, cases, cares
b) range - (mad) anger; lump - (fruit) plum; sauce - (reason) cause;
   palms - (light) lamps; inch - (part of the face) chin